# Pluto
## The Dwarf Planet

By Greg Roza

**Gareth Stevens**
Publishing

**Please visit our Web site, www.garethstevens.com. For a free color catalog of all our high-quality books, call toll free 1-800-542-2595 or fax 1-877-542-2596.**

**Library of Congress Cataloging-in-Publication Data**

Roza, Greg.
 Pluto : the dwarf planet / Greg Roza.
   p. cm. — (Our solar system)
 Includes index.
 ISBN 978-1-4339-3837-5 (pbk.)
 ISBN 978-1-4339-3838-2 (6 pack)
 ISBN 978-1-4339-3836-8 (library binding)
 1. Pluto (Dwarf planet)—Juvenile literature. I. Title.
 QB701.R69 2011
 523.49′22—dc22
                                    2010012652

First Edition

Published in 2011 by
**Gareth Stevens Publishing**
111 East 14th Street, Suite 349
New York, NY 10003

Copyright © 2011 Gareth Stevens Publishing

Designer: Christopher Logan
Editor: Greg Roza

Photo credits: Cover, back cover, p. 1 European Southern Observatory; p. 5 Shutterstock.com; p. 7 (Earth) NASA; pp. 7 (Pluto), 11 (Pluto) NASA/JPL; p. 9 NASA, ESA and G. Bacon (STScI); p. 11 (moon) NASA/JPL; p. 11 (Pluto cutaway diagram) Lunar and Planetary Institute; pp. 13, 17 NASA, ESA, H. Weaver (JHUAPL), A. Stern (SRI), and the HST Pluto Companion Search Team; p. 15 ESO/L. Calçada; p. 19 NASA, ESA and M. Buie (Southwest Research Institute); p. 21 NASA/JHUAPL/SwRI.

Printed in the United States of America

CPSIA compliance information: Batch #CS10GS: For further information contact Gareth Stevens, New York, New York at 1-800-542-2595.

# Contents

**Boldface** words appear in the glossary.

## Say Hello to Pluto

Pluto was discovered in 1930. For 76 years, Pluto was considered the smallest and most distant planet in the **solar system**.

# Our Solar System

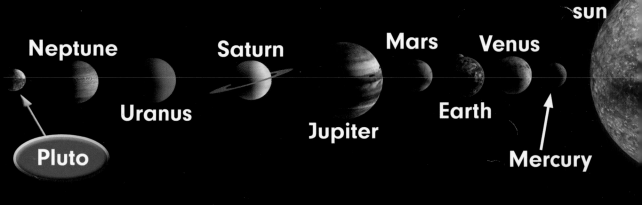

Neptune

Uranus

Pluto

Saturn

Jupiter

Mars

Earth

Venus

Mercury

sun

In 2006, scientists decided Pluto wasn't big enough to be called a planet. They called it a "dwarf planet."

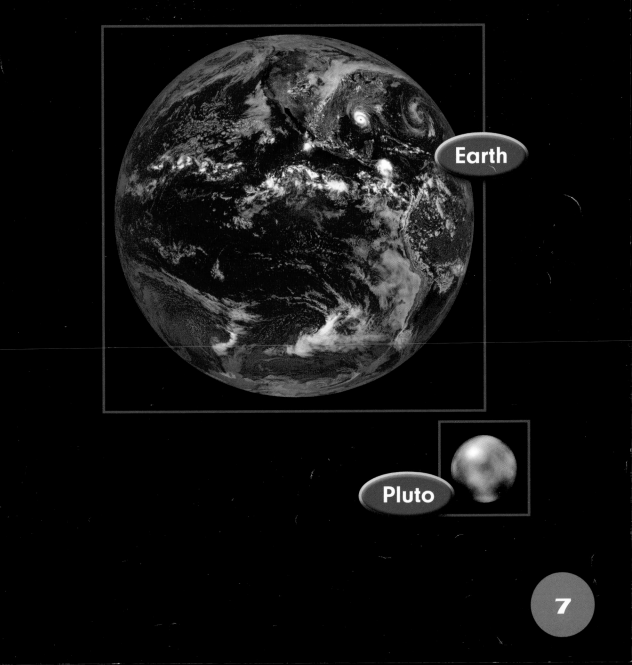

Earth

Pluto

## What Is a Dwarf Planet?

A dwarf planet is a very small planet. Besides Pluto, scientists have found several other dwarf planets in our solar system.

moon of Pluto

Pluto

moon of Pluto

9

## Small, Cold, and Rocky

Pluto is smaller than Earth's moon. It's covered in a thick **layer** of ice. Beneath the ice, Pluto has a rocky center.

Pluto

Earth's moon

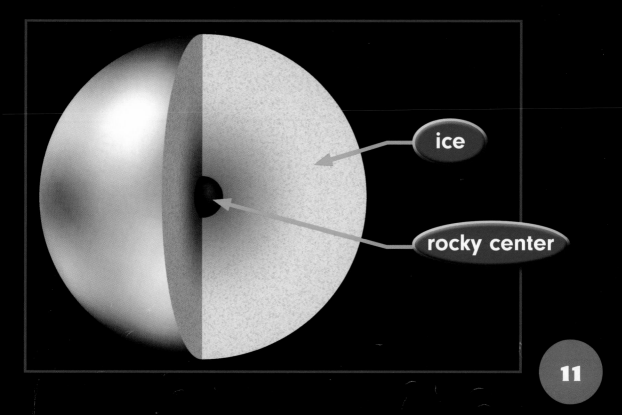

ice

rocky center

## Pluto's Moons

Pluto has three moons. Pluto's largest moon—Charon (KEHR-uhn)—is about half the size of Pluto. Nix and Hydra are much smaller.

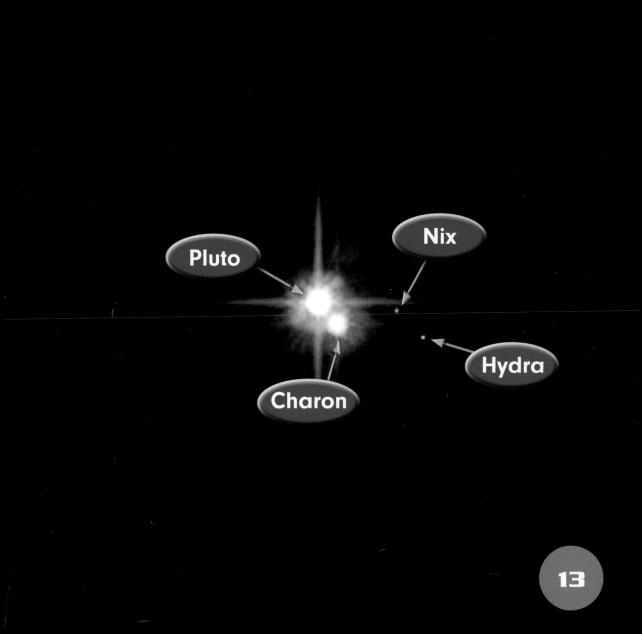

Pluto

Nix

Charon

Hydra

13

## Way Out There

If you could stand on Pluto, the sun would look like a big star. That's because it is so far away. Pluto takes about 248 years to **orbit** the sun just once!

## Hard to See

Pluto is so small and far away that it's very hard to see. This picture of Pluto and its three moons was taken with a powerful **telescope**.

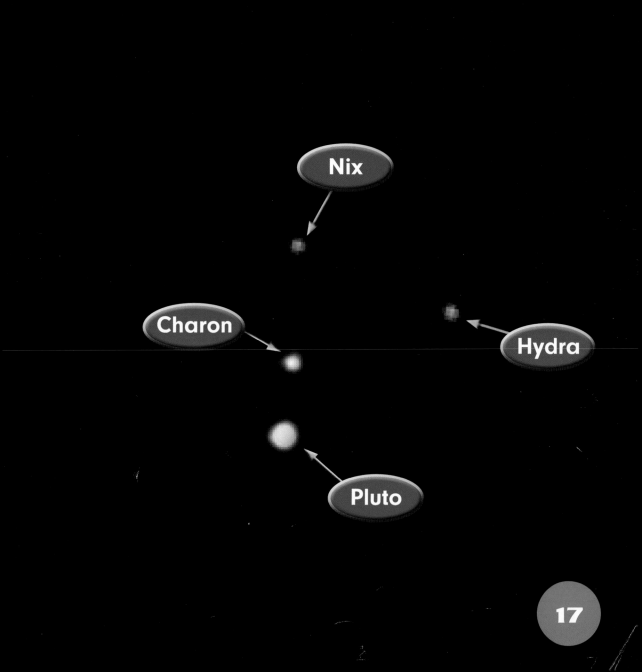

Nix

Charon

Hydra

Pluto

Since it's so hard to see Pluto, scientists aren't sure what it looks like. This is the clearest picture we have of Pluto.

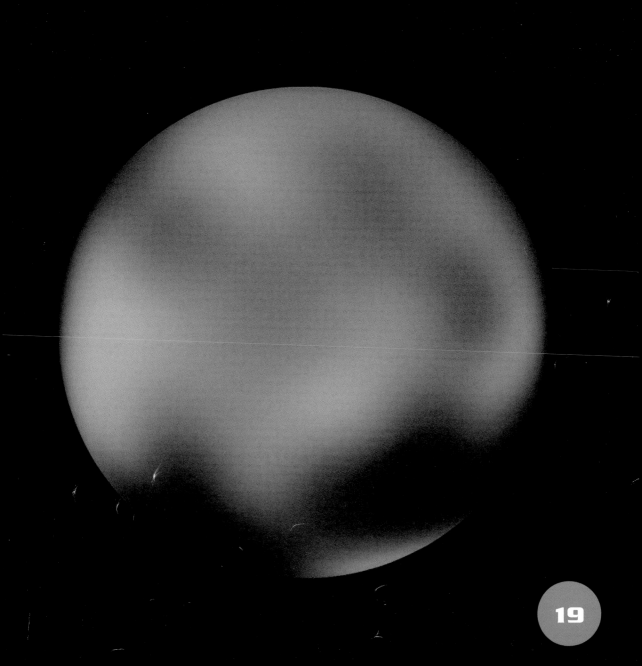

19

## Visiting Pluto

Scientists want to know more about Pluto. In 2015, a **probe** will travel closer to Pluto than any spaceship has before. It will take the first clear pictures of the dwarf planet.

probe

21

# Glossary

**layer:** a thickness of something lying over or under another

**orbit:** to travel in a circle or oval around something, or the path used to make that trip

**probe:** an unmanned spaceship

**solar system:** the sun and all the space objects that orbit it, including the planets and their moons

**telescope:** a tool used to make faraway objects look bigger and closer

# For More Information

## Books

Kortenkamp, Steve. *Why Isn't Pluto a Planet?* Mankato, MN: Capstone Press, 2007.

Loewen, Nancy. *Dwarf Planets: Pluto, Charon, Ceres, and Eris.* Minneapolis, MN: Picture Window Books, 2008.

Taylor-Butler, Christine. *Pluto: Dwarf Planet.* New York, NY: Children's Press, 2008.

## Web Sites

**Ask an Astronomer for KIDS!—Pluto**

*coolcosmos.ipac.caltech.edu/cosmic_kids/AskKids/pluto.shtml*
Learn more about Pluto by reading questions and answers about it.

**Hail King of the Ice Dwarfs!**

*spaceplace.jpl.nasa.gov/en/kids/pluto*
Read interesting facts about Pluto and see helpful diagrams.

**Publisher's note to educators and parents:** Our editors have carefully reviewed these Web sites to ensure that they are suitable for students. Many Web sites change frequently, however, and we cannot guarantee that a site's future contents will continue to meet our high standards of quality and educational value. Be advised that students should be closely supervised whenever they access the Internet.

# Index

## About the Author

**Greg Roza** has written and edited educational materials for young readers for the past ten years. He has a master's degree in English from the State University of New York at Fredonia. Roza has long had an interest in scientific topics and spends much of his spare time reading about the cosmos.